JN 979.2 Giis
40448
23.00

THIS LAND CALLED AMERICA: UTAH

D1518489

CREATIVE EDUCATION

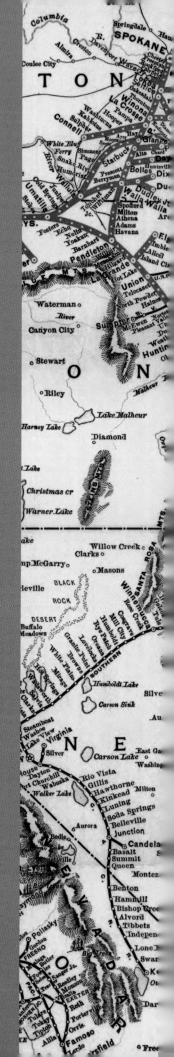

Published by Creative Education

P.O. Box 227, Mankato, Minnesota 56002

Creative Education is an imprint of The Creative Company

www.thecreativecompany.us

Design by Blue Design (www.bluedes.com)

Art direction by Rita Marshall

Book production by The Design Lab

Printed in the United States of America

Photographs by Alamy (Anthony Arendt, blickwinkel, Danita Delimont, Tom
Till), AP Images (Douglas C. Pizac), Corbis (Bettmann, George H. H. Huey,
George D. Lepp, David Muench, Galen Rowell, Pete Saloutos, H. David Seawell,
Scott T. Smith, Tim Thompson, Tony Waltham/Robert Harding Imagery),
Getty Images (Marc Adamus, John G. Mabanglo/AFP)

Copyright © 2010 Creative Education

International copyright reserved in all countries. No part of this book may be
reproduced in any form without written permission from the publisher.

Library of Congress Cataloging-in-Publication Data

Gish, Melissa.

Utah / by Melissa Gish.

p. cm. — (This land called America)

Includes bibliographical references and index.

ISBN 978-1-58341-797-3

1. Utah—Juvenile literature. I. Title. II. Series.

F826.3.G57 2009

979.2—dc22   2008009526

First Edition

9 8 7 6 5 4 3 2 1

This Land Called America

UTAH

Melissa Gish

Utah

MELISSA GISH

IN THE EARLY FALL, A WARM BREEZE BLOWS THROUGH A RED ROCK CANYON. SHARP ROCK FORMATIONS TOWER HIGH ABOVE A DUSTY TRAIL. RIDERS ON HORSEBACK TRAVEL ALONG A RIDGE. THEY ADMIRE THE STUNNING HOODOOS THAT SURROUND THEM. THESE TALL, THIN ROCKS WITH LAYERS OF RED, ORANGE, AND WHITE WERE CARVED BY MILLIONS OF YEARS OF WIND AND WATER. THE RIDERS LOOK DOWN INTO THE CANYON AND SEE PEOPLE ON MOUNTAIN BIKES. THEY LOOK UP TO A STEEP CLIFF AND SEE A PERSON CLIMBING THE SHEER ROCKFACE. WITH HUNDREDS OF HIGH RIDGES AND DEEP VALLEYS, UTAH'S CANYON COUNTRY IS A MAGICAL PLAYLAND.

YEAR

1650 The Utes become some of the first Indians to use horses, which were introduced by the Spanish.

EVENT

Western Freedom

PEOPLE FIRST SETTLED THE LAND NOW KNOWN AS UTAH
THOUSANDS OF YEARS AGO. ITS EARLIEST INHABITANTS WERE
THE FREMONT AND ANASAZI PREHISTORIC PEOPLES. THEY
RAISED CORN AND MADE POTTERY AND BASKETS. BOTH
CULTURES DISAPPEARED ABOUT 700 YEARS AGO. THEY LEFT
VARIOUS FORMS OF ROCK ART, SUCH AS PETROGLYPHS AND
PICTOGRAPHS, ON THE ROCK WALLS OF THE CANYONS.

Later, Ute and Goshute American Indians lived in Utah. They hunted deer and buffalo, and they fished in Utah's many lakes. Beginning in the 1500s, explorers from Spain began claiming land west of the Rocky Mountains, including Utah. In 1776, a group of Spanish explorers traveled from Mexico (which was owned by Spain) to Utah. Two of these explorers were priests, Silvestre Vélez de Escalante and Francisco Atanasio Dominguez. They were the first Europeans to visit the area.

The priests wrote about Utah in their diaries. Their stories told of the natural wonders they had seen. Soon, more explorers came from Spain. Fur traders came from Mexico (which took control of Utah after winning independence from Spain in 1821). And American frontiersmen such as Jedediah Smith traveled across the Rocky Mountains to find routes that pioneers could use.

Early Indians such as the Anasazi made their homes in Utah's cliffs (opposite), but later tribes such as the Ute roamed on horseback (above).

YEAR

1776   Priests Silvestre Vélez de Escalante and Francisco Atanasio Dominguez become the first Europeans to visit Utah.

EVENT

- 7 -

Jim Bridger was a famed mountain man, trapper, scout, and guide from the 1820s through the 1860s.

By the early 1800s, the fur trade in Utah had grown. A man named Jim Bridger helped establish trade routes through the area. He led many pioneers through the West. In 1824, Bridger became the first frontiersman to see Utah's Great Salt Lake.

The area around the Great Salt Lake soon attracted Mormons, members of a religious group that was formed in the 1820s. Among the early Mormons' beliefs was that men could have many wives. People who did not agree with this and their other beliefs drove Mormons away from every place they tried to settle. In 1847, thousands of Mormons moved to Utah in search of religious freedom.

At the time the Mormons arrived in Utah, the United States and Mexico were fighting over the land in the Mexican-American War. In 1848, the war ended with the U.S. forcing Mexico to give up much of its land, including Utah. The Ute, Paiute, and Navajo tribes did not want whites settling on their land. Fights broke out between pioneers and Indians. Despite this, more white settlers poured into the area, including about 70,000 more Mormons. They founded Salt Lake City. On January 4, 1896, Utah became the 45th American state, and Salt Lake City was named its capital.

In the late 1800s, large Mormon families often lived in small, log homes on Utah's frontier.

YEAR
1841 Eighteen-year-old Nancy Kelsey becomes the first white woman to journey through Utah.
EVENT

On May 10, 1869, the Union Pacific and Central Pacific railroads were joined in Promontory, Utah.

Cowboys, farmers, and other workers established many cities across the new state. Dams and power plants to create electricity were constructed on the Beaver River and other waterways. The government passed laws to protect Utah's wild places. Zion National Park was established in 1909.

In 1912, a contest was held to design the state's capitol. A man named Richard Kletting won the contest. The building was made of beautiful white rock dug out of Utah's Little Cottonwood Canyon. The capitol's dome was covered in Utah copper.

Industry boomed across the state in the early 1900s. Flour mills operated for 24 hours a day. People mined for natural resources such as coal, iron ore, copper, silver, and gold. Salt Lake City became a major stop along the First Transcontinental Railroad, which connected America's East and West coasts. Utah was building an exciting future.

Salt Lake City's streetcar system, which began running in 1872, helped people move about the bustling city.

YEAR

1858   Gold is discovered in the mountains of Utah, luring thousands of prospectors.

EVENT

Shaped by Time

THE WESTERN STATE OF UTAH HAS STRAIGHT BORDERS. ITS NEIGHBOR TO THE WEST IS NEVADA. ON ITS NORTH SIDE ARE IDAHO AND WYOMING. COLORADO IS TO THE EAST, AND ARIZONA LIES TO THE SOUTH. A CORNER OF NEW MEXICO TOUCHES UTAH IN THE SOUTHEAST. UTAH'S VARIED LANDSCAPE BOASTS MOUNTAINS, VALLEYS, DESERTS, AND THE GREAT SALT LAKE.

Northeastern Utah is covered with mountains such as the Wasatch and the Uinta (*YOO-in-ta*). Kings Peak, in the Uinta Mountains, is Utah's highest point. It is 13,528 feet (4,123 m) tall. Trout and bass are abundant in mountain streams and lakes. Mule deer, elk, and moose roam the mountains' pine forests.

Millions of years ago, glaciers cut through Utah's landscape. They carved the sharp canyons and sloping valleys of the Colorado Plateau. The Plateau covers most of southern and eastern Utah. This high, flat land has an elevation of more than 11,000 feet (3,350 m).

The Colorado River weaves through the Colorado Plateau. The river is swift and features many rapids. The red rock walls of the river gorge are high and steep. Giant cottonwood trees grow along the water's edge.

Rocks in the Great Salt Lake may be encrusted with salt (opposite), but the water in the High Uintas Wilderness is salt-free (pictured).

Two railroads meet at Promontory, Utah, completing the First Transcontinental Railroad.

In 1963, a dam was built on the Colorado River, forming Lake Powell in southeastern Utah. Almost 100 different canyons in Utah were flooded by the lake. Coal mining is an important industry east of Lake Powell and up through the mountains. Companies drill for oil in southeastern Utah as well.

Southern California's Mojave Desert reaches into the corner of southwestern Utah. The northwestern part of the state is an area of small mountains and wide valleys called the Great Basin. Farmers raise cattle and sheep and grow wheat, sugar beets, and other crops there.

The Great Salt Lake is located in the Great Basin. The size of the lake changes, depending on the amount of rainfall the area receives. Its record low was in 1963, when it covered only 950 square miles (2,460 sq km). But the record high, in 1987, was 3,300 square miles (8,550 sq km).

Herds of sheep are found in southwestern Utah (above) as well as in the Great Basin; in the southeastern part of the state are Lake Powell and the Glen Canyon National Recreation Area (opposite).

1896   Utah becomes the 45th state on January 4.

The Great Salt Lake is briny, which means that it contains a large amount of salt and other minerals. Factories around the lake take these minerals out of the water. The minerals are then used to make fertilizers, industrial salt, and detergents.

The Bonneville Speedway consists of two racetracks that are marked out for motor sports in the Salt Flats.

The Great Salt Lake Desert lies west of the Great Salt Lake. About 4,000 acres (1,620 ha) of hard, flat salt beds cover the center of the desert. These are known as the Bonneville Salt Flats. People once mined the minerals, but today the land is protected. Now people use the flats for speed racing.

Utah's climate varies. West of the mountains, summers are dry. In the Salt Lake City area and the surrounding mountains, rainfall is heavier. And except in the hot desert, temperatures all across the state rarely climb above 80 °F (27 °C).

A view from outer space shows part of the Great Salt Lake and the vast expanse of white salt beds next to it.

Fewer than five inches (13 cm) of winter snow may fall in the west. But up to 500 inches (1,270 cm) may fall in the mountains each year. There, the temperature can drop to -50 °F (-46 °C) in the winter. The rest of the state usually stays above 20 °F (-7 °C).

YEAR

1914   Automobile speed racing gets its start at the Bonneville Salt Flats.

EVENT

- 17 -

Innovation and Tradition

MORE THAN 80 PERCENT OF THE PEOPLE WHO LIVE IN
UTAH ARE WHITE. PEOPLE OF HISPANIC AND LATINO
DESCENT MAKE UP ABOUT 11 PERCENT OF THE POPULATION.
VERY FEW AMERICAN INDIAN, ASIAN AMERICAN, OR
AFRICAN AMERICAN PEOPLE LIVE IN UTAH.

About 60 percent of Utah's population is Mormon. The Mormons' Church of Jesus Christ of Latter-day Saints dominates Utah's culture. Leaders of the church meet with state government officials to discuss issues and policies. Mormons favor traditional practices and ideas based on the church's beliefs. For this reason, the state is known for its conservative views.

The first Mormons to settle in Utah were led by a man named Brigham Young. In 1847, he became the president of the Church of Jesus Christ of Latter-day Saints. He guided people as they built their settlements. Young became the first governor of the Utah Territory. He also encouraged the U.S. government to build the First Transcontinental Railroad through Utah.

Workers quarried rock from the Little Cottonwood Canyon (opposite) for use in building the Mormons' Salt Lake Temple (above).

YEAR

1928 Bryce Canyon, named for pioneer Ebenezer Bryce, is established as a national park.

EVENT

Steve Young began his NFL career in Tampa, Florida, but was most known for his years with the San Francisco 49ers.

In the mid-1800s, Young established the Mormon Tabernacle Choir. The choir continues to sing and inspire people today. All of its members are Mormon. The choir began singing for radio broadcasts in 1929 and has appeared on television since the 1960s. In 1981, U.S. president Ronald Reagan called it "America's Choir." People all around the world buy the choir's music today.

One of Brigham Young's descendants is athlete Steve Young, a former National Football League quarterback. He was born in Salt Lake City in 1961 and had a long and successful career. In January 1995, Young was named the Most Valuable Player of Super Bowl XXIX. In 2005, he was inducted into the Pro Football Hall of Fame.

The 360-member Mormon Tabernacle Choir presents a weekly radio broadcast entitled Music and the Spoken Word.

YEAR

1929 The Mormon Tabernacle Choir makes its radio debut on stations throughout the country.

EVENT

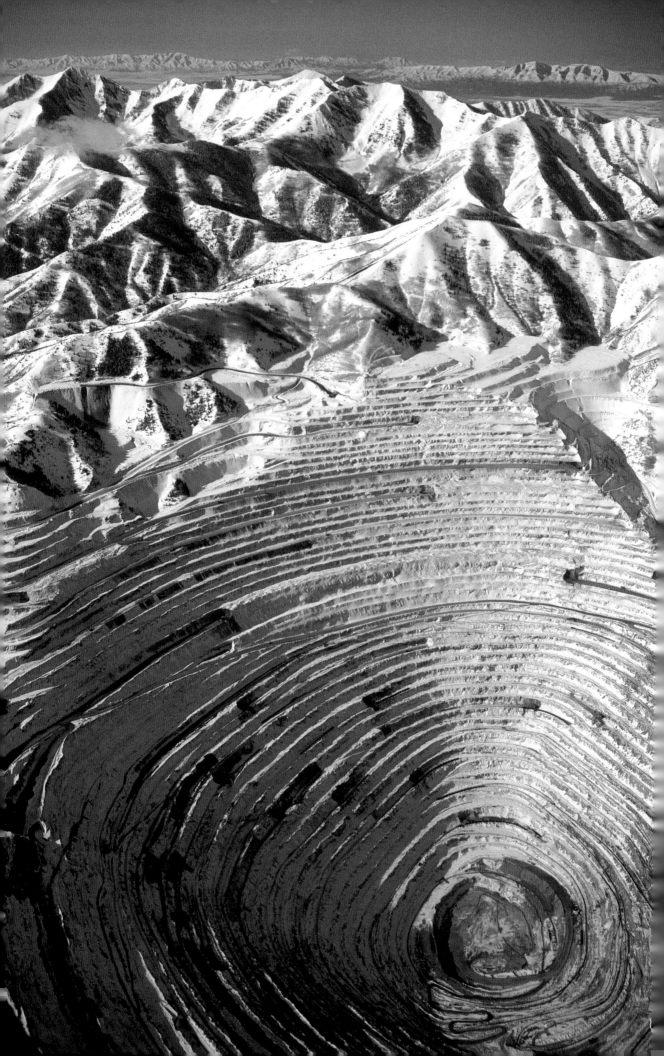

Another Mormon family from Utah, the Osmonds, formed a singing group in the 1970s. The seven siblings were known worldwide for their harmonious pop music. One brother, Donny, joined his sister, Marie, to host a musical television show in 1976. Most of the Osmonds continue to perform today, either by themselves or as a group.

Utah State University's Space Dynamics Laboratory contributes to research done in aerospace technology.

Utah is an innovative state, with schools and companies dedicated to aerospace technology. Factories build parts for satellites and space shuttles. Rockets are also constructed. Even parts for U.S. Air Force fighter jets are made in Utah.

Gold fever is alive in Utah, too. The chance to find gold brought many people called prospectors to the state in the 1800s. Some gold can still be found among the reserves of another metal called copper that is mined in the central part of the state. Utah pulls more than 15 tons (14 t) of gold from its mines each year.

At the Bingham Canyon Mine, an open-pit copper mine near Salt Lake City, gold ore is also extracted.

YEAR

1934 Hundreds of wells and dozens of dams are created after Utah suffers the worst drought in its history.

EVENT

Brine shrimp

Another industry that has remained strong for more than 100 years is situated on the Great Salt Lake. Billions of brine shrimp, tiny animals that grow no larger than half an inch (1.3 cm) long, are harvested from the lake to make fish food. The brine shrimp industry funds a research program to study the environment of the Great Salt Lake and its shoreline.

Just as Utah's industries have remained strong over time, so have the traditions of the state's American Indian people. The Ute people hold powwows and perform a special Bear Dance every year. The Navajo, Paiute, and Goshute tribes also keep their culture alive through festivals and powwows.

Near the Great Salt Lake, where brine shrimp (above) are found, several northern Utah Indian tribes gather at certain times of the year to dance in colorful costumes at powwows (opposite).

YEAR
1956   The Colorado River Storage Project is established to manage water, control flooding, and provide electricity.
EVENT

Natural Art

UTAH IS A LAND OF STUNNING ARCHITECTURE, ADVENTUROUS PEOPLE, AND NATURAL BEAUTY. VISITORS TO SALT LAKE CITY CAN GO DOWNTOWN TO TEMPLE SQUARE AND SEE THE MANY BUILDINGS THE MORMONS BUILT THAT ARE ASSOCIATED WITH THEIR CHURCH, INCLUDING THE SALT LAKE TEMPLE. COMPLETED IN 1892, THIS ORNATE BUILDING HAS THREE SPIRES FLANKING EACH END OF THE TEMPLE.

Nearby, the modern-looking EnergySolutions Arena is home to the National Basketball Association's Utah Jazz. One of the most famous basketball stars of all time was Utah's John Stockton. He was a member of 10 All-Star teams and two U.S. Olympic teams. Fans loved him. When he retired in 2004, the street in front of EnergySolutions Arena was renamed John Stockton Drive.

The 400-foot (122 m) Castleton Tower presents a challenge to rock climbers in the desert near Moab.

Utah provides outdoor sports and adventure as well, from rock climbing and mountain biking to fossil hunting. Thousands of fossils have been discovered in Utah. Dinosaur National Monument, in the far northeastern corner of the state, includes a massive glass-enclosed rock wall that contains hundreds of exposed fossils.

Salt Lake City offers cultural attractions as well as architectural interests such as the Salt Lake Temple.

South-central and southeastern Utah boast rare and ancient sandstone formations. Much of the land there is protected by the government. In Arches National Park, more

YEAR

1976   The musical variety show of Utah natives Donny and Marie Osmond first appears on television.

EVENT

Some petroglyphs found on Newspaper Rock in southeastern Utah were carved more than 800 years ago.

than 2,000 sandstone formations have been sculpted by the wind. These incredible-looking rocks have names such as Fiery Furnace, Delicate Arch, and Tower of Babel.

Nearby, Canyonlands National Park is 528 square miles (1,368 sq km) of canyons and arches. Most of the park has no roads. Hikers and drivers in off-road vehicles can follow trails to see an area of massive red-and-white layered sandstone pillars called the Needles. The Great Gallery is a canyon wall covered with rock paintings of ghostlike figures, people, and animals. Experts think the drawings could be 3,000 to more than 9,000 years old.

In southwestern Utah's Bryce Canyon and Cedar Breaks, people can see fantastically shaped rock columns called hoodoos. Minerals in the rocks called iron and manganese make the hoodoos red, orange, yellow, and purple. These colorful pillars stand up to 200 feet (60 m) tall. The local Indians called Cedar Breaks the "Circle of Painted Cliffs."

Almost 1,000 years ago, Indians built stone towers in southeastern Utah. Their ancient ruins stand at Hovenweep

Along with its famous hoodoos, Bryce Canyon National Park is also known for its natural stone bridges.

YEAR

1996 President Bill Clinton sets aside land to create Grand Staircase-Escalante National Monument.

EVENT

- *28* -

2002   Salt Lake City hosts 2,399 athletes from 77 nations for the Winter Olympics.

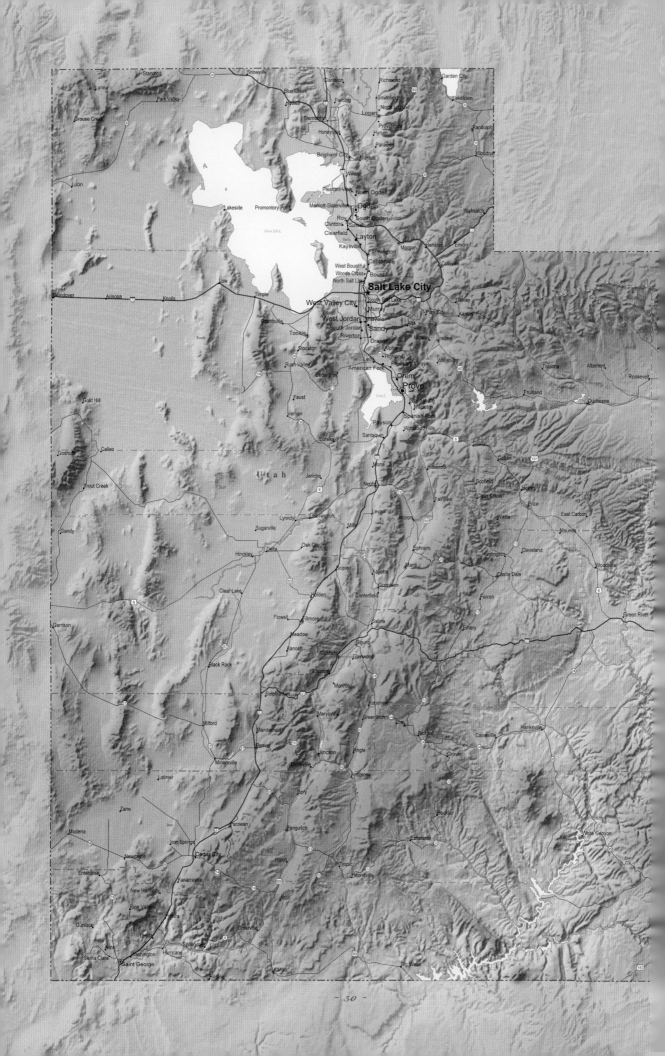

QUICK FACTS

Population: 2,645,330

Largest city: Salt Lake City (pop. 180,651)

Capital: Salt Lake City

Entered the union: January 4, 1896

Nickname: Beehive State

State flower: sego lily

State bird: California gull

Size: 84,899 sq mi (219,887 sq km)—13th-biggest in U.S.

Major industries: agriculture, mining, tourism, aerospace technology

National Monument along the border with Colorado. Nearby is Natural Bridges National Monument. Its three sandstone bridges were formed by streams that cut through the canyon walls millions of years ago.

Because of Utah's unique landscape, filmmakers often choose to shoot scenes in the state. Hollywood actor Robert Redford fell in love with Utah when he filmed the movie *Butch Cassidy and the Sundance Kid* in 1969. The movie *The World's Fastest Indian* and some parts of *Pirates of the Caribbean: Dead Man's Chest* and *Pirates of the Caribbean: At World's End* were shot at the Bonneville Salt Flats. And the rock scenes in *Galaxy Quest* were filmed in Goblin Valley State Park. Perhaps the most filmed natural landmark in Utah is Monument Valley, where tall, red rock formations rise up from the flat desert landscape, creating a stunning backdrop.

Utah is a land of varied scenery and ever-changing weather. The people of Utah value their natural and cultural heritage, and they keep their Old West traditions alive. But they also work hard to expand their industry and technology to secure a strong future for their state.

BIBLIOGRAPHY

Griggs, Brandon. *Utah Curiosities: Quirky Characters, Roadside Oddities & Other Offbeat Stuff*. Guilford, Conn.: Globe Pequot Press, 2007.

McRea, Bill, and Judy Jewell. *Moon Handbooks: Utah*. Emeryville, Calif.: Avalon Travel, 2004.

Repanshek, Kurt. *Hidden Utah*. Berkeley, Calif.: Ulysses Press, 2006.

Whitley, Colleen. *From the Ground Up: A History of Mining in Utah*. Logan: Utah State University Press, 2006.

Zwinger, Ann. *Portrait of Utah*. Portland, Ore.: Graphic Arts Center Publishing, 1999.

INDEX